CLOSE
to the
BONE

CLOSE
to the
BONE

DAVID LAMPE

Ink Drawings
by
GABRIELA CAMPOS

Introduction
by
A.F. MORITZ

EXILE
editions

singular fiction, poetry, nonfiction, translation, drama and graphic books

Library and Archives Canada Cataloguing in Publication

Title: Close to the bone / David Lampe ; ink drawings by Gabriela Campos ;
    introduction by A.F. Moritz.
Names: Lampe, David, 1941- author. | Campos, Gabriela, illustrator. |
    Moritz, A. F. (Albert Frank), writer of introduction.
Description: Poems.
Identifiers: Canadiana (print) 20200200038 | Canadiana (ebook)
    20200200046 | ISBN 9781550968811 (softcover) | ISBN 9781550968828
    (EPUB) | ISBN 9781550968835 (Kindle) | ISBN 9781550968842 (PDF)
Classification: LCC PS3612.A6325 C56 2020 | DDC 811/.6—dc23

Canadian sales representation:
The Canadian Manda Group, 664 Annette Street, Toronto ON, M6S 2C8
www.mandagroup.com 416 516 0911

North American and international distribution, and U.S. sales:
Independent Publishers Group, 814 North Franklin Street,
Chicago IL 60610 www.ipgbook.com toll free: 1 800 888 4741

For Ruth

Contents

CONFLUENCES:
DAVID LAMPE'S *CLOSE TO THE BONE*

"Confluence," a word he uses, is basic to David Lampe's poetry. In "Castlerigg Stones," Lampe's poet is visiting "38 slate pillars / on a low hill above the confluence / of Nabble Creek and river Greta" near Keswick, Cambria – the English Lake District – Wordsworth country. In comes a "reverent herd of cattle," duly then surrounded themselves by a busload of tourists taking photos.

> *Neither the reek of cow*
> *flop, nor the* click click click *of*
> *cameras, can sully this sublime site.*

The confluences here are of the "sublime" and the ordinary, of the perennial and the passing and, most profoundly, of the pure and the sullied. What we came for, splendor, remains mysteriously intact within the heart at the same time that it is equally inhabited by all distracting minutiae of our existence, the smells, the sounds and busyness of others, our reactions to and opinions of it all. Not either/or but both/and: true life is elsewhere, and here; we are elsewhere and here.

Beyond the words "sublime site" and the tiny description, "38 slate pillars," Lampe doesn't characterize the site's sublimity, doesn't try to produce its parallel in words. This is an aspect of the confluence Lampe achieves in his deep-running, quiet-and-lovely-surfaced poems. The poems give the everyday "surround" in its constituent detail. Reek. Cow flop, the Americanism for shit carried by the American in his mind into rural England. The cameras and tourists put before us by their tiny precision sound: *click*. The poem's sound patterning is as concrete as its narrative-descriptive realities. The two long *e*-s prefiguring and giving the smell, the *rEEk*. Then the *k* of "reek" initiating the tiny explosive continuity, the *k* sounds, of insistent annoyance: reek, *click click click*, cameras...fading away at "can" into the sublime, the sibilant suggestion of the Ideal in the three *s*'s and the two bright *i*'s rising out of the mud/*merde*/dullness of "sully."

The only detail given to the sublime is the symbolic gestural one, "upward." Thus here, just where it is needed, Lampe transitions from the modern American sublime of concrete details evoking/enclosing spirit to the greater, Juan Ramón Jiménez-type sublime of "naked poetry," the emotional-intellectual-spiritual reality presented in its bare purity of possible symbolization, with no concession whatever to the decorative, elaborative hunger and tendency of modern poetry and the modern mind. The Castlerigg Stones are a sublime site/sight, and you must site and sight it for yourself, in yourself. No description is going to provide it if you can't. In furtherance, I bring Lampe's tiny poem, "Musical Blessing":

Never a soloist, I blend,
become part of a sacrifice
of the self, a note by note

release of energy into
Dante's "sweet
harmony of Paradise."

Lampe's subjects are his careers as a poet and a medi-
evalist, his experiences as a traveler (in Ireland, locale
of many personal and poetic associations; to Cistercian
sites in Europe and the dark crypts of northern Protes-
tantism; to neolithic sites; to many American hunting
blinds and fishing holes), his memories of an Iowan
childhood and family, his friendships with such as John
Montague, Hayden Carruth, Judson Boyce Allen, Joel
Oppenheimer, Eric Haugaard; and especially his friend-
ship with the love of his life, his recently dead wife, Ruth.
These make up the simple, generous substance of his
book. But in saying this, we have to keep in mind that the
two "careers" of poet and professor (of medieval studies
and of creative writing at SUNY College at Buffalo) means
the confluence of the deep past of culture, the sublime
visions of such as Dante and the Cistercian mystics,
with contemporary experiences and the poet's personal
history.

There was not too long ago a concentration by critics
and scholars on the "American sublime," which is almost

an anti-sublime, along the lines mentioned above: the finding of the highest in the ordinary, the locating of presences and hints of the eternal – "intimations of immortality" – in the intimate and quotidian. Lampe is an excellent, original poet in this tradition. How "American" is it? It seems like the substance of Romanticism, in fact, as my quotation from Wordsworth implies, and as a reading of "Michael" or "Poems on the Naming of Places" or "Nutting" will confirm. In American Romanticism, Whitman recommends the poetry of attention to the specificity of every person and place and fact, and yet dominantly (although there *are* poems and passages like "Sparkles from the Wheel" and "A Farm Picture") his vision of the particular is a sublime and general vision: "all are supreme."

Whitman is the prophet of the actual poets of the particular who were to come, and it took a while for them to begin coming. So they did. Something like the selection of Ted Kooser as the U.S. Poet Laureate (2004-06) can be taken as acknowledging and honoring this. But it's arguable that the poets of the particular came as much and as early – the first six or so decades of the 20th century – in Ireland and England and France and elsewhere, as in America: Rilke, the sequence Hopkins-Hughes-Heaney, Edward Thomas, R.S. Thomas, Apollinaire, Ponge, Follain, Machado, Ungaretti… Lampe's friend Montague is an example in Ireland, as shown by some lines from Montague that Lampe quotes in an epigraph: "A flowering, flaring bank of rhododendron / Fathomless darkness, silent raging colour..."

Nothing could be further in tone, it seems, from the sublimity of Whitman than the modest succinctness and reportorial minuteness of Lampe, but the filiation is there.

Close to the Bone contains far too much of people and places to cover in brief remarks, so let me leave exploration to the reader – it will be her and his consistent joy – and close on the fact that Lampe himself is fully aware of this confluence of the here-and-now and the eternal, and even seems to discuss its nature, sometimes using the great Irish poet William Butler Yeats as his foil.

In one poem, Lampe quotes Yeats's famous mystical lyric, "The Song of the Wandering Aengus," in which the poet fishes with a berry and catches a silver trout that turns into a "glimmering girl / With apple blossom in her hair," who vanishes and prompts a never-ending quest. Lampe's poet, by contrast, says he learned to "jig my minnow" over an "eighty-foot deep strip / mine."

The poem, "At the Fishing Hole," from the American wording of its title, down through its entire substance, sings a specific fact of person and place, which at the same time is an *ars poetica*, which at the same time is a vision of the unseen in the seen, a vision which Lampe distinguishes from yet joins with the vision of Yeats. Lampe fishes with "No hazel rod, / no silken strand: instead, / a sonar sounding device / that hooked me a golden / trout..." Not a silver trout, like Yeats's. A trout that is just a trout, and thus pure gold, the transformation of dross that the magicians seek. It's found in the real. Lampe's poetry does not take him to the magical fruit of the unseen reality of day and night, but at the same time it does. He tells us that his trout was no glimmering girl with apple blossoms in her hair,

> *no*
> *girl who called me by my name,*
> *but instead, became*
>
> *the silver apples of the moon,*
> *the golden apples of the sun.*

Does he mean that his trout was different from Yeats's in that it did not send him forever to seek that magical fruit? Or does he mean that it was different from Yeats's in that it actually *turned into* that fruit? The syntax has it both ways. The humble ending of the poem with nothing of his own, with a direct quotation from Yeats, like the direct quotation from Dante that ends "Musical Blessing," expresses and affirms Lampe's never-a-soloist self-placement in the sublime love of the past and present of poetry, and of the places and people that are his.

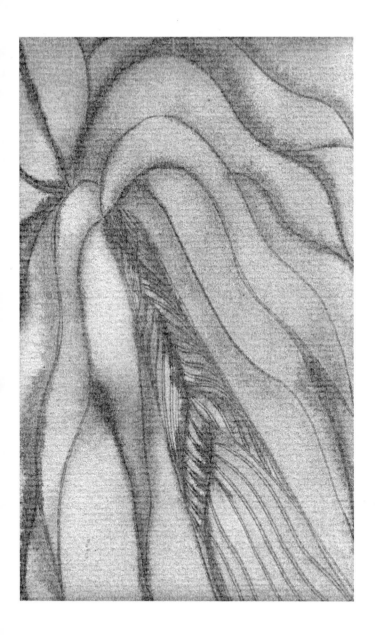

After Cataract Surgery

They look like trees to me
But they are walking about
—MARK 8:24

And when I woke early
that May morning
birds sang

and when I stepped into
the backyard and removed
the bandage from my eye

the colors of a cardinal
flared, were crisp as he flew
from a boxwood hedge

to a forsythia bush
whose leaves of shimmering
light were beheld

through a shudder of tears.
Yellow scales fallen,
the trees walked.

Legacy

—a bracelet of bright hair—
—JOHN DONNE

Two years after her death
I open an
oblong paisley box

containing my mother's
braided auburn hair,
a candy-cane ribbon, and

a crinkled faded photo:
"Me before my first haircut
when my hair was bobbed."

I learn such pigtails
can be made into a wig
for children battling cancer.

She would approve:

bracelets of bright hair
are now about the bone of
another twelve-year old.

Modern Times

I was a boy…

My grandparents took me
to Trumbull Lake to fish
for bullheads and perch

which we later plated
with potato salad and
a schluck of Grandpa's beer.

The almost-only time
I took my young sons fishing
was to cast spinners

in an over-stocked pool
at Allegany State Park
where frenzied

sunfish, all skin
on the bone, attacked
even bare hooks.

Crusader's Credo/Joys Of Jihad

Slaughter them all, God knows his saints!

—ARNOLD, ABBOT OF CITEAUX

[afterwards, Archbishop of Narbonne (1209)]

We follow Him as best we can,
the smashing, the rending,
is Our Lord God's work,
idols and graven images
all holy deeds, all destruction
blessed according to
His commands.

Below the Skin

Your bank of flaring rhodo-
dendron against a glacial corrie!
On close investigation you discover
the absence of undergrowth is brought on
by acid from those glistening leaves
burning out everything below.

In Kerry, below the skin
where a malignant darkness rages,
they're not so sentimental,
they burn out rhododendrons
by using flame-throwers.

Hunting, October '03

The Roberts' home place,
Fenced-in and farmed for four
generations, despite a bucket
brigade, burned down.

The asbestos-sided
house, the barn, granary,
the sad rickety corn crib,
the rank odor of hog shit

(which poisoned
the groundwater), all gone.
Johnnie Roberts lost an eye
to a night-flying ember.

And here I am, hunting
with my son on this fallow
land, spent red casings,
No. 6 shot, all around

my feet. I have not yet
lost an eye, only a way
of seeing down along
these empty roads.

Shattered Head, Cluny (Paris)

O sacred head,
the brain cleaved away

by iconoclasm.
This mouth,

though mute,
still has its say:

Plus Oultra!

Poetry Slam

Trust Americans to turn
poetry into a sport

missing only thirty-
second timeouts
for commercials and bad officiating.

I stayed thru eight
performances,
the last by a certain Will B. Heard

who was as subtle as her name.
Still, no harm no foul.

North of Sioux Narrows

Fishing for walleyes
that summer before
I went to college

the blue water was so
limpid we could watch
the fish approach and

strike the frogs
we used for bait.
Though no fish

ever tasted better
than those we caught,
cleaned, and cooked on

that Precambrian stone
shore, it was almost too
easy, so we filed the barbs

off our hooks to give
them a fighting chance.
Years later when I first

tasted frog legs in
Bill Zuber's Restaurant
I understood why

those walleyes
attacked with such
abandon.

Saint Knud's, Odense

"Danes don't like God very much anymore."
—Nils Holger Petersen

So this is
Northern
Protestantism:

Severe
ground-chill
of a white-washed

crypt, a priory
altar to a saint
martyred,

his ivory
ribs, yellow
pelvic bone,

mounted in
a glass-enclosed
case

on a brick
base of
similar yellow.

On the Hunt

1

Sunrise as bald
eagles skim over
the graveled trout stream...

A bright yellow
blur of railroad boxcars
crosses the Thompson River bridge...

A screaming star explodes
above the sulfur loads, a bleeding
salmon in its talons...

2

Up by Sunk Grove
with its burr oak, bog,
and opaque open

water, a proud tom
gobbles from the wooded
draw, the warble of a bird

in the long grass. Two hens
pecking. And then,
as the tom is about to re-

enter the woods, a single
shot at fifty-two yards
drops him.

Austrian Excess

But the fat and strong I will destroy
—EZEKIEL 34:16

After Schloss Schönbrunn
(excessive as it sounds),
we're taken to the Mayerling
chapel of "the little flower,"
St. Theresa (the serrated edge
of Cistercian piety) that had
once been a Hapsburg hunting lodge
where, amidst horned trophies,
the syphilitic crown prince had
shot his lover, then himself.
"A continuing tragedy,"
our tour guide explains.
"He might have saved the empire,
spared us two world wars."

An even sadder fact:
Not all Hapsburgs shot themselves.

Zwinger Gallery, Dresden

[Allied "saturation bombing, Feb. 13-14, 1945,
scarred this baroque Florence on the Elbe]

Twin marbles
on either side
of this moated
courtyard,
his tam-

bourine
beater
broken
in his fist,

her black-
ened flute
touching her
char-
red lips.

Muttersprache

She washed my hair
with soft, scented cistern water,
anointed my head
with shampoo.

"What does fuck mean, Mommie?"
Source of goodness and tough
mercy, and she told me, blunt
as blunt could be:

"A man and a woman
put their privates together
like a bird with a bird, a bee
with a bee, to make a baby."

We dwell
in the words
of our mothers
all the days of our lives.

Carrowmore, Dolmen 7

As the rain slants in
I shelter under the portal
of this broken circle
of stones, tip my

silver flask and offer
a drop to the earth,
it's as good as I've got.
When the rain stops

I startle a red-haired
woman by *hallooing*: "When I die,
I'll have one of these
dolmens over my grave."

Heading off heavy-booted
toward a herd of cows,
she says, "Sure, now,
keep it simple, nothing ostentatious."

Smor Och Brod

Stillness of an awkward
silence between us
at Shango's Sunday brunch

of cornbread and butter,
so I blurted out a bedtime
prayer in mangled *barn*

Svensk taught me fifty
years ago by Grandma Alice,
"The kindest lady a child

in his night terrors could
ever know." Tommy Olafson,
my guest from over home,

chortled, "Ja, dat's old archaic,
prayer talk is always
good talk." The winter sun

loomed brighter
as we took up our silence,
this time with a smile.

Wild Wales

On a cool early evening,
Basil, our host in
North Wales,

power mows his small
grass field
as we, on the stone

veranda behind Ship
Cottage, try nosing
a brace of crisp Pinot

Grigio that will
complement a Somerset
baked brie,

jalapeno jelly,
and sea salt water
biscuits.

What's in a Name

In the occluded
corner of a Dublin

snug my friends, Mont-
ague among them, ex-

plain a sore truth:
"There's trouble enough

in your name." Only
now, at 59, I learn

that going lampe
along the Liffey means

I'm loopy.
"Even so," I reply,

"where I come from
we call that being Irish."

St. George's Basilica

A plundered pietà,
heads, arms, even
the legs are gone.

Yet, amidst a cluster
of dried flowers, crimson
and gold, a mother's hand

clutches her son's
cold side where
the wound still bleeds.

Cottonwoods

On the Iowa plains, cottonwoods
sacred to the Lakota,
take root near deep ditches

along gravel roads like the one that
serviced our family farm
where each summer

webs of seed spirited out
like spider's silk into the air
around our house that'd been built

of uncured cottonwood beams like
those under our "old kitchen" floor
that in time came crashing down,

pulpy, perhaps because they'd
grown too fast. Years
later, my son showed

me an ancient tree
down among old slate markers
near Spoon River where

what I thought was an oak
turned out to be two cottonwoods
in twisted embrace around a stone,

no silk in the air at this time
of year, only a few
leaves clinging to the

names of those long since
returned to dust
in that dank yard.

Elders

1

Great-uncle Elmer gave me his buckram-bound,
11th edition *Britannica* along with a sheaf of home-
printed, deckle-edged photos of our prairie clan,
and the construction stages of his house, which he
had built for his fiancée only to learn on the party line
she had run off and married a young college man.
All he ever said about that was, "Never trust a young
man who chews tobacco." He never once reminded
my mother that she had handed him the phone.
Instead, being bookish by nature, he warned her,
"Never let your son read H.G. Wells."
Years later when I told him that I had, he just shook his head.
He died in the house he'd built, mouth open, not saying
a word, his hand resting on the closed family Bible.
"He shouldn't have been a farmer," my mother said,
never suggesting what Elmer should have been.

2

Great-uncle Charlie was a storekeeper who lived
in his wife's "home place," a ragged frame house
across the road. Everyone knew that Emma held the
purse strings to what little money they still had. She had
good teeth, and smiled a lot, and wore a cloth hat
that had blue flowers in its band. He was a spare,
white-haired man who never wore a hat, even when
it was raining. He did wear a Panama straw hat when
he was painting. He painted in oils and liked to chew
Spark Plug tobacco when he was at his easel.
He never told me not to chew tobacco, nor did he worry
about what I read. He himself did not read books. And he
didn't keep good business books either, so they lost their store.
Charlie didn't seem to mind much. He had his studio,
an old granary that smelled of turpentine, corn, and dead rats.
He'd set up his easel and paint houses, meadows,
and woodlands on 9 x 12 canvases stapled to pine stretchers
he made himself. He was stung one day by a hornet
when he unreeled a hose from among overgrown ferns
near his easel. He died of shock. Nobody but my mother
kept his paintings. She had loved Charlie.
The granary and the house are long since gone.

3

My grandfather H.W., on the paternal side, loved
to make sandwiches of roast beef cut thin, tidily
trimmed of any sweet fat. He sliced the beef in exact
lengths to cover Grandma Mary's homebaked pumpernickel.
He never praised her for her bread or her cooking.
"Almost right this time, Mom," he would say. She never
showed any resentment, never batted an eye. For a while I
thought he must have trimmed a whole lot between them,
but then I decided that if she was hurt, she'd found a way
to best him by slathering her bread beneath the beef
with head cheese. "That's what I read in a magazine about
how to do it," she told him in the same tone she used
when they argued about driving too close to the center line.
"I suspect you're afraid of going off the edge of the road,
H.W., dear." Mind you, he always laughed when she
said that, so I never was quite sure what to make of them
and how they loved each other.

Family Values

Saw this big-hat dude
in an Elmwood brew-pub
chug-a-lug his Bud Light
from a bottle, chaw down
on his jerk chicken,
ignore his young sparrow-breasted wife
and smirk as he swaggered
out in his high-heeled
roach killers, leaving her
with the backpack
baby and a diaper-bag
that had a fluorescent decal
on it, Pro-Life.

A Game That Can't Be Won

1

In Ireland, I played
pitch and putt,
until I hit my ball

on top of a stone wall.
Returning my rented
clubs, I asked what

I should have done
and was told without a smile
"Hit it from there."

2

And then home, jet-
lagged, to play a front-
nine with my two sons.

Light-headed, feeling strangely
loose, I chipped in from
the fringe and sank long putts

and actually broke 40.
At the tenth hole, I swung
and fell down. One son

said, "Hit him where
he lies." The other son
cried, "Fore."

Spoil a Child

Thy rod and staff, they comfort me
—Psalm 23:4

At mother's wake
Arlyn Youngberg tells me how
his first-grade teacher, Miss Peterson,

strapped him hard.
He told my brother
the same story, how he

had taken off into
a field in winter
during morning recess

and had come back in
britches wet to the knees
from wading in snow.

Miss Peterson called him
to the cloakroom, told him to
hold out an open hand

which she struck
with a length of belt.
It stung real hard, Arlyn

remembers seventy years later.
"But mostly because we really loved
your mother, our Miss Peterson."

Dies Irae, Dies Illa

"Who is Joe Green?"

As I listen to Verdi's
Requiem—"Live
from the Met"—all

that excess of vocal
display...

My first choir tour
comes back to me...

Town of Brewster,
Minnesota, a Presbyterian
proud people

who put us up post-
concert, a kind of
stiff-necked

graciousness. Only
gradually did I
understand (a 17-year-

old freshman) that
these folks, so like my own
family, weren't ready

for songs of sorrow
in Latin by a man
named Verdi...

"Some things,
after all, are
just too Catholic."

Oxford Coldness

I.M. Judson Boyce Allen (1933-1985)

That graceful Tennessee glide asking
"What you doin' heah?" is the warmest
voice I've heard in Oxford's Bodleian.

"North Oxford for drinks—
call when you get lost." And I did,
confusing North and South Parade.

Bristol Cream my gift
though it was Laphroaig you poured as
I fumbled with your half-calf biblical commentary.

After we drove back under a cold Oxford rain
we looked in at your college
for several pints of best-bitter.

And paused beneath the eerie dome lights
of Shelley's translucent marble shrine,
even more epicene than Michelangelo's

recumbent Christ. The best-bitter
had overcome our Protestant regret at the absence
of the Holy Blessed Virgin in our lives as

we left that unreal city of sleeping spires
and walked over Magdalen Bridge.
When we reached my hotel

I was aching cold and soaked through.
You had your umbrella and no time
for a nightcap, no time for an awkward embrace.

The only warmth I ever found in chilly
academic Oxford, the only voice that echoes still,
has a Tennessee glide, "What you doin' heah?"

Oh blithe spirit, would that we could again cross that
bridge and share a cup of kindness in a world
you once made best when all seemed bitter.

Spring Is Here

A sure sign of middle-
America springtime
is the coming back

of Sandhill cranes
to Kearney, to the mighty
Platte River where,

as my mother said,
"They sing
and sometimes

they even
dance, maybe because
they're nervous

at being alive
all over again or, even
better,

maybe they're in love."

Moving On

You whispered to me:
"I'm going to be moving on."

(Before we had a radio in our car,
you and Grandpa, to while away the time,
argued about driving too close to the center line

on the 71 to Excelsior Springs
where we learned to chew milk
and I almost drowned in a saltwater pool.)

Then years later, here you are calling
on a winter's evening, to ask
do you have my folks' number?

You whisper again, "I've dialed my parents,
the old Pomeroy exchange,
but no one answers."

"Mom, I wish we could call,
but they've been dead for years."
All you said was, "Oh,"

and that you loved me, and then,
"You too will dial up the dead, you know.
You too will want to move on."

In Rehearsal

1

Playing God in
Everyman on a tour
of Iowa Presbyterian

church towns…pre-
destined to declare, "I perceive
here in my majesty,"

seated from up
on the highest rough
rafter of this lakefront

shelter house, "how
all creatures to me
be unkind," trying

to shout down a blind-
drunk roustabout of rowdies,
if only temporarily.

2

There I was holding
Willy Loman's samples suitcase,
rehearsing how it is

to die of a salesman's
suicidal optimism
when Gooch, my college

director, driving me around
a country road toward,
Storm Lake, handed me—

seeking counsel and consolation—
his own suitcase of sorrow:
his wife had tried to kill herself.

3

The pride of my young
life, Ruth, stung by love,
became my prairie bride,

vowing honor and obeisance.
Later, about to perform
my translation of the Middle-

English morality play, called,
as it happens, *Pride of
Life*, she balked, refused

the role of the servile, whining
Queen. She didn't stomp her
foot, just said, "No. No way

under the sun." What was I to say?
That it was not life, just a play?
Either way, our rehearsal was done.

Drumcliffe Churchyard, Sligo

Cast a cold eye
On life, on death.
Horseman pass by.
—W.B. YEATS

Being a pale
Protestant, I know
how to cast a cold eye

as I pass by church
sycamores and lichen-
laced gravestones.

Mind you, if I'd had a
horse and a
gold watch chain,

life would have been
different,
and death, too.

"Cajun Tex in Old Orleans"

His leather Stetson hat,
his pearl-handled Colt, holstered,
snakeskin boots, Cuban heels,
silver buckle in the shape
of a *fleur-de-lis*...

Bien clair...
What else could his roots be?

As we were about to board
the last train,
I mumbled, "Git along, Tex,
allons y, allons y
little doggie."

Harbour Haven, Ballydehob

*"These stories, stripped as they are of the fashionable
and modish, give us — at least for a moment — that
peace which is necessary for survival."*
—ERIC HAUGAARD on Hans Christian Andersen

By the pebbled shore outside Eric's
house, spindly-legged, grey-
plumed cranes, tower above
the slack tide's slime.

"The stupid gulls can't stand
them," Eric explains, "all their *skree,
skree, skree* as they try to force
the cranes down to their knees."

Baroque concertos fill
his domed, sky-lit library.
Warmed by a second bottle
we discuss Hoeg and Kierkegaard

and groan and tut about a fool
who'd *skreed* on about Rothko,
"a painter you may not have heard of."
I am shown a signed Max Beerbohm

and an early edition of Parkman,
"that I first read and borrowed
from Ezra Pound's library." Twilight closes in,
there's a chill as the sun drops down,

and back at the wheel of my hired car
I can see Eric in the rear-view mirror,
long-legged, looking flush in a grey Aquascutum,
the tide coming in as he waves from the shore's edge

My Father and the Atomic Bomb

August 7, 1980, Cork City:
As I crossed Patrick Street
in the shadow of that stern

prohibitionist, Father Mathew,
all black in his bronze gaiters
a Ban-The-Bomb panhandler

rattled his collections can at me
and cried, "The only comedian
not running for president

this summer is Bob Hope—
Cheques accepted, Yank."

                ★

My father worked
on building the atomic bomb.
As a boy I knew he rode

every day after every day
on his bicycle to work
at the "Lab" only a few blocks away

from our Howard Street home;
his only preening was to polish
to a high blue tone our "Hi Ho"– the

family Chevy coupe; he told me how
a non-consuming fire burned, and how,
with a machinist's craft and skill,

he made precision carbon crucibles;
and how an explosion moved a brick
wall (intact) three full feet and how

the Ames Fire Department had to sign
affidavits declaring they had seen
nothing; and how Frank Spedding,

whose eyes twitched sideways,
as he left for Bavaria, told Dad,
"If ever this is used anywhere

in the world, you'll know."
He did, I guess, though he never
talked about "this" even when

I was a man. Which I was
on a sunny afternoon in the Iowa
State gym with my Mom

when I attended a calling out
of Dad's name at a solemn ceremony
where I accepted on his behalf

a commemorative pin, a silver *A*
against that familiar cloud set in
a cluster of bronze olive leaves.

The pin found its place
on top of his bedroom bureau
in his cufflinks and tie clasp

dish in our family house,
now itself reduced
to char and ashes.

Home Fires

Corn is our gold.
—Iowa legislator

On a crisp November Sunday,
after a Reformation service
in our rural Iowa church,

we drove two miles
and went to the upstairs
bedroom in our home place

that no longer
exists where my father taught
me to tie the same

Windsor knot that I taught
my sons to tie in that
same room, yes, a simple

cross-over and drop
loop, which was and
is as corny

as it sounds,
one of those family
ties that binds.

Suppression

Ivan Hastings, child of the deaf mutes
who rented Emiline Schneider's farm,
attended my country church and was

in my second-grade class.
He was clumsy with language,
his consonants misshapen.

When our teacher called him out,
he stammered, or was silent,
and so she drew

a chalk circle on the board,
forced him for hours to keep
his nose in that circle. His

uncomplaining silence
increased, her rage.
Her filed thumbnail pinched

blood from his long earlobe.
His suffering, his mute grace
leads me to let loose a long

suppressed shout of defiance.

At the Fishing Hole

*I dropped the berry in a stream
And caught a little silver trout.*
—W.B. YEATS

I learned to jig my minnow
under ice that sheeted an
eighty-foot deep strip

mine. No hazel rod,
no silken strand: instead,
a sonar sounding device

that hooked me a golden
trout that was no
glimmering girl with apple

blossoms in her hair, no
girl who called me by my name,
but instead, became

the silver apples of the moon,
the golden apples of the sun.

Homage

For Joel Oppenheimer (1930-1988)

Over ten years ago
I tried to write a tribute
to your flat reading voice
which brooked no shit
as it found in the ordinary
an occasion for singular wit.

Thinking about how
my mother embarrassed me
when I was a child
I asked my youngest son
if I had ever embarrassed him.
Without pause he said
that I had introduced you
to his class at City Honors and it was
bad enough to have a parent
who brought poets to his school, but worse,
after my introduction,
I turned to sit down
and finding no chair

sat on the floor at your feet.
He shuddered
remembering that moment.

And yet, my friend, master,
I would do it again.

"What Is So Rare as a Day in June?"

I can still see that
big smiling Swede
in a small North-

woods Minnesota
town proudly
holding up his

stringer of wriggling
walleyes and without
guile or a wink telling

me he had caught
them in the dark lake
with his own

bare hands while
the stars shone out
at noon.

Kilcolman Castle

An Irish fact is what they tell you in Ireland.
—HUGH KENNER

1

Driving for four hours
because I'm stubborn—
because I could hear Montague
cackle, "You couldn't find it?"

Then, before dusk, there was
Kilcolman, close by the house
of the old lady who in the morning
had warned me to "mind the gap."

2

Well, anyway, who wants to read
The Faerie Queene these days,
five books too long? And who
has ever suffered regret

at the last books being burned
(also Spenser's child, a sorrow)
in this Kilcolman Castle? Let ivy
and cattle undo the walls at last.

3

Six months later Hayden Carruth
tells me to ignore
the drunken snake twisting
through those stanzas

and to trust the *Queene*
for what it is "as you find it"—
archaic, intricate but accessible
in its "narrative thrust."

Castlerigg Stones

July 2003
Keswick, Cambria

Castlerigg Stones, 38 slate pillars
on a low hill above the confluence
of Nabble Creek and river Greta,

walking distance from Wordsworth's
Dove Cottage, a circle of standing
stones surrounded by mountains

as we are surrounded by a reverent
herd of cattle as they are surrounded
by off-loaded Japanese tourists.

Neither the reek of cow
flop, nor the *click click click* of
cameras, can sully this sublime site.

Songs My Father Loved

At separation, the father sings a song to his chick.
It is the only way they will know one another.
                              —March of the Penguins

General Butterfield's lights-out signal, "Taps" is 24 notes
based on a 3-drum taps pattern.
                              —Bugel Book (1862)

1

(1947)
As we drove on Sunday afternoons
in our Chevy coupe, the tappets clicking,
you sang "Pack up your troubles
in your old kit bag and smile,
smile, smile." I smiled. "When you get older
we'll buy you a bugle and you can play 'Taps.'"

2

(1956)
He asked me to play
"Reveille" or "Hail to the Chief"—both of which
were in my yellow bugle call book. I blew
a discordant Stan Kenton riff, and being
a patient man, he nodded, and
then nodded again, and said,
"OK, Dave, that's the band
practice music, now play 'Taps.'"

3

(1996)
At his funeral, I read the obituary,
the eulogy, and even a poem.
I was fine, no tears, until uniformed
American Legionnaires, men
who had also seen Lily Marlene underneath the lamplight,
stood crooked and gaunt, singing, "Pack up your troubles…"
and I heard him say, "OK, Dave, play 'Taps,'"
but I couldn't because I'd packed up
my trumpet in an old trunk
after I'd stopped listening to the blare of Kenton's big brass.

Musical Blessing

Never a soloist, I blend,
become part of a sacrifice
of the self, a note by note

release of energy into
Dante's "sweet
harmony of Paradise."

John Montague Died Today

I recall how
we'd walked out
one evening
to a sports bar
on Chippewa St.
so old and *ofay*
to the core
it still
had a painting on its walls
of Cassius Clay

where John
in his Jameson cups
and full academic regalia after
receiving an honorary degree,
told me, "The English lost
their poetry when they

not only gave up
the true
religion, but took
the adverb to heart."

*

At a summer
campus reading,
almost an hour late
and roaring drunk,

he charmed
the audience
into forgiveness

by chanting a poem
about a love aborted
"as snow curled in
on a cold wind"—

a poetry so "close
to the bone that
it hurts and helps…"

Like a Lark Singing in the Open Sky

> *We made a lark into a giant bird who will travel*
> *the skies of the world long after our names are forgotten,*
> *or confused, or cursed down.*
>
> —WARWICK, in *The Lark*

> *Your job is to create memories.*
>
> —BOB FINK, Hospice Chaplain

Ruth's strong mother
lived to be 98,
so I assumed

Ruth would survive me
since I'm almost two years older.
But, alas, that was not to be.

We'd met in *MND*, Shakespeare's
great comedy about marriage, but
I remember her best as

Joan of Arc in Jean Anouilh's
The Lark in which I played the
miscreant bishop who burned her.

At Nebraska Ruth played
a witch girl in a stage
version of Bergman's

Seventh Seal and was burned
again. I joked that it
was typecasting.

1 Kinder

When we moved to Buffalo
it did not take Ruth long to challenge
the "god damns" (Joan's catchword

for English ruling authority).
And her work left its mark
on our block, on Parkside

and even (I'm told) on City Hall.
She did not always (perhaps wisely)
take my advice but did heed Jeff's

and retired early from teaching
(after her student debate team won the city
championship) and took on the role of

grandmother. One of her proudest
claims was her part in the lives
of each of our seven grandchildren.

2   Kirche

Next to family was her faith.
During our 46 years in Buffalo
we worshipped in two Lutheran congregations,

Our Savior's and St. Paul's—
in both Ruth was a council
member, teacher, and leader.

During her nine-month illness we were
amazed by the "clouds of witness,"
those angels of whom

we had been unaware who
emerged from churches,
from our community,

from our families,
and from among our dear friends.
They have been the

bread and wine that has
sustained us and for which
we are profoundly grateful.

3 Klagen

The song of the lark,
that exhilarating voice
of liberation through

service to and with others
resounds for me
here today

and echoes beyond
this world
and into the next.

"You Must Remember This"

for Ruth

The sophisticated artistry
of Stan Kenton's
rhythm section

embellished by
loudly dissonant
brass—those

resonant trombones,
edgy trumpets
and mellow

mellophoniums,
provided the wall of sound
for our first real date.

Seventy miles
on the road but worth it
to expunge

the puerile pulp of
egregious Elvis and
Jailhouse Rock

which you saw for
a second time
in two days.

Years later Iowa
City friends asked
Kenton to dedicate

"Peanut Vendor" to us in
Lincoln. We've always
assumed he did
though we were
delayed by
cocktail lushes

who wouldn't leave
(grad school leeches)
and so arrived to hear

"Malagueña," the very
song that got me fired
from an idiot Iowa

radio station when I played
it rather than Mantovani
or the Melachrino Strings.

Never mind, fundamental things
apply and we would
always seek consolation

in the joys of early memory,
in songs never out of date
that welcomed us anew as lovers.

So no matter what the future
twists or denies,
these remembered melodies

summon up our love
in all its glory
as time goes by.

Hospice

Hospice – a place to pause on your journey.
—Wilma Newberry

What I do trust is mystery, I trust confusion.
—Jennifer Chang

We confuse—
in this age of high tech,
of labor-saving

devices that waste time,
keep us from
silence and solitude—

the two terms
"hospice"
and "hospital."

Though syllable
cousins there's
powerful

difference between
a frantic
emergency room

(a too often
necessary place, alas)
and a quiet

hospice room
where we
wait,

a pause
in the clock
on our journey.

1

I experience
all these
confusions

when Ruth
completes
her crossing

8 a.m.
August 8
2015.

2

I had never been
present at the death
of anyone I loved—

my father suffered
a sudden
nocturnal heart attack,

my mother slipped away
as I was driving to
reach her,

a hundred
miles away.
But, thank God,

I was with Ruth
for those last
moments of mystery.

3

My medievalist friend,
Judson Allen,
a PK from Tennessee,

the last time
I saw him told me,
"I could almost

thank God for
my cancer since
it gave me time

to prepare
an answer."
To what?

For whom?
I was at a loss.
But after piecing

together final plans
with Ruth, I began
to understand.

"I'm not afraid of death,"
she said. "It's just
getting there that's scary."

4

Those last moments
were hard—
her staggered

breathing, the dry
retch—they were
desperately hard.

Morphine did not
help *kommst du*
susse Todesstunde.

5

Despite Bach's pietistic
plea or later
overblown Germanic angst

it was sweet
and bitter at best.
Sweet since

she had avoided
the indignities
of cancer—

incontinence, in-
coherence,
intolerable pain—

bitter for me since
I had lost the love
and center of my life.

6

So now when
asked,
"How are you?"

I respond,
"Fine."—
a white lie

unless I
detect
true concern.

Then I say
I often cry
when reminded

of Ruth
by a chance word
overheard,

by a perfume
that brings her
scent back to me.

I fall to weeping,
and weep,
and weep

and Oh…

Tree Planting

—*September 12, 2015*

In *Table Talk*, Martin Luther
was asked what he would do
if he knew that today

was the end of the world.
"Plant a tree,"
he said, "for the dead."

For life-long Lutherans
like Ruth and me that affirmation
of ordinary perseverance

has been very important—
indeed provides the model for
what we have tried to do

in our community and
today in this Olmsted Park
where Ruth's family plants this tree.

As Willa Cather's
tragic Bohemian Marie
says in *O Pioneers!*,

"I like trees because they
seem more resigned
to the way they have to live

than other things do."
She explains, "I feel
as if this tree knows

everything I ever think of
when I sit here. When
I come back

I never have to remind it
of anything; I begin
just where I left off."

We of Ruth's family
look forward to
sheltering together

under this sycamore in
Olmsted's and our
own dear Delaware Park.

Quandary

Who would have thought
two Iowa farm kids
would not

merely survive
but thrive
in a rust-belt

border town,
even
contribute,

we were told,
to the integrity
of local matters

by merely
living out the
plain-spoken

probity we
learned
at home?

St. John's Cemetery (Albert City, Iowa)

Five generations of Lampes,
enough to hallow any field,
reaching back beyond easy memory.

I have stood in this place for
parents and grandparents
and stand now for my wife.

Early on, Ruth said
she did not fear death—
only the trying to get home safe.

Now that is over
and we return to Iowa,
our place of origin,

early days and
our education—
source of values

we never lost
but instead tried
to re-establish in

another community
we came to love
and to serve.

As our favorite novelist
Willa Cather put it,
"Fortunate country,

that is one day to
receive hearts like
[Ruth's] into its bosom

to give them out again,
…in the rustling corn,
in the shining eyes of youth."

Even Our House Mourns

I know it's a "pathetic fallacy"
to impose our emotions
on the world around us,

that it's an unreliable
subjective response
to our surroundings,

even more particularly
to the house my wife and
I lived in for 45 years.

There certainly must be
some rational explanation
for the strange events

of this last month—
the electrified
Gone with the Wind

lamp that fell to the floor,
shattering into
fragments after

20 years of subdued
light in the corner.
Or the sudden

rush of water
from the third-floor
radiator that brought

down the ceiling
in our bedroom.
I know that old houses

don't shed tears,
don't throw things
crashing to the floor.

These are human responses,
the things I would do,
not the house.

Yet it seems to have
a will and pain
of its own.

I foolishly thought
that after her death
the house

and the pain
were mine
and mine alone.

Acknowledgements

To my colleagues and friends in the Buffalo poetry community who have indulged me and from whom I continue to learn. To Marsha Boulton whose careful proofing caught several embarrassing errors. To my friend Barry Callaghan who has inspired, aided and abbetted me in several poetic ventures. To Michael Callaghan who makes wonderful books, and to Gabriela Campos who helps make them beautiful.

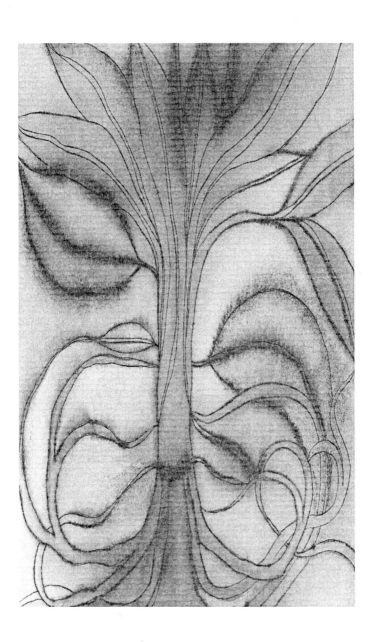